Making Friends

A Book About First Friendships

words by AMANDA McCARDIE   pictures by COLLEEN LARMOUR

This is the story of Sukie and how she made friends.
It begins when she moved with her family
and started at a different school.

At first she felt lonely, sad and small ...

7

Then some of her new classmates started being friendly. Each time, Sukie felt warm inside and wanted to be friendly back. One said hi to her during P.E.

One passed her a hula-hoop before they all got taken.

One helped her find her way when she was lost.

Now Sukie knew that friendliness was catching! So she smiled when she met a shy classmate by the coat pegs one morning.

The next time they met was easier,

and the next time was easier still.

Sukie and Joe were making friends.

When Sukie saw Poppy playing bounce and catch,
she plucked up her courage
and asked to join in.

Soon Poppy's friend Stan
joined in as well — and
friendship grew out of a game.

Sukie hoped all her friends would like each other. She brought them together lots of times, and soon she could see they did.

They were friends making friends with the friends of their friends!

But things weren't always easy for Sukie.

One day, she asked a boy called Mikkel if she could help him with his jigsaw, but Mikkel said no, he wanted to do it by himself.

Sukie's skin felt crinkly with embarrassment.

She hurried away to find Poppy.

For a while they played quietly, then Sukie told Poppy what had happened. It was a sort of telling called "confiding", which meant Sukie trusted Poppy — to be kind, to care how Sukie felt, and not to tell other people about it.

"Sometimes I want to play on my own as well," said Poppy.

They laughed, and the crinkly feeling faded away.

A few weeks later, Sukie's classmate Alex
made fun of her red hair.

Joe was ready to stand up for her straight away.

He said calmly to Alex, "Stop being mean to Sukie."

Thanks, Joe.

READ

Everyone stopped laughing, even Alex. Her joke didn't seem very funny after Joe had called it mean. Joe was a brave, loyal friend that day.

At the end of term, Sukie's class put on a gym display – then Joe rushed off too quickly at the end.

He felt silly, but his friends were there to support him.

Sukie found that she and her
friends were alike in lots
of ways.

They all enjoyed meeting up,

playing

and laughing,

chatting,

messing around

and sharing lunch.

In other ways they were different. For instance, Stan didn't worry the way Sukie did.

Sukie was late sometimes, but Joe was almost always on time.

When Poppy was happy, she stood on her hands.

When Sukie was happy, she made people laugh.

And Sukie *was* happy. Not every minute, all the time – just warm and safely happy deep inside.

Free to be open, to be themselves,

Sukie and her close friends

grew closer every day.

AUTHOR'S NOTE

This book isn't about things going wrong between friends — although sometimes they do.

It's about things going *right*.

I wanted to explore and celebrate some of the good things about friendship. You might recognize some, or think they're wrong, or want to add more ... and that's fine.

Maybe there are friends in your life just now, maybe not. Either way, I hope this book will help you to think about what it really means to be a friend.

INDEX

* You'll find someone being kind on almost every page!

For Julia, with love – A.M.

For Rose and Nina – C.L.

and with so many thanks to Jo Gaskell

First published 2020 by Walker Books Ltd
87 Vauxhall Walk, London SE11 5HJ

2 4 6 8 10 9 7 5 3 1

This book has been typeset in AnkeSans

Printed in China

British Library Cataloguing in Publication Data: a catalogue record for this book is available from the British Library

ISBN 978-1-4063-8756-8

www.walker.co.uk

WALKER BOOKS
AND SUBSIDIARIES
LONDON · BOSTON · SYDNEY · AUCKLAND